Able To Stand

Dr. Daryl G. Donovan

Fairway Press
Lima, Ohio

ABLE TO STAND

FIFTH PRINTING 2009

FOURTH PRINTING 2008

THIRD PRINTING 2007

REPRINT DECEMBER 2006

SECOND PRINTING 2006

FIRST EDITION
Copyright © 1996 by
Dr. Daryl G. Donovan

Library of Congress Catalog Card Number: 95-62011

ISBN 0-7880-0643-6   PRINTED IN USA

Dedication

I dedicate this book to my parents, Bob and Thelma Donovan, vessels God used to give me life ... and to point me to Him ... and to every Christian who is bruised and bleeding from various falls or stumbles, who has a passion to be able to stand.

Acknowledgments

With deepest gratitude to:

Elaine, my gracious wife who encouraged me to complete this book, who served as first editor, who stands as my godly helpmate.

Rebekah, Kristen, Benjamin, and Kay who have taught me much about what it means to be a child of God.

Karl and Dottie Ellington, in-laws who have treated me like a son. Typists and "set-up" crew.

First Christian Church, Nevada, Missouri, who gave love and support through the stormiest time of my life . . . allowing me to get to a place to learn how to stand.

Central Baptist Theological Seminary, who provided a place to retreat to for the completion of this book.

GOD, My Heavenly Father, Who loved me enough to sit me down and teach me to stand.

Sanibel Community Church, who has faithfully proclaimed the message of the abundant life found only in Jesus.

Introduction

Jesus said to Simon Peter, "Simon, Simon, behold Satan has demanded permission to sift you like wheat; but I have prayed for you that your faith may not fail; and you, when once you have turned again, strengthen the brothers." (Luke 22:31-32 NAS)

The sifting to which Jesus referred was Peter's thrice denial after the crucifixion. Jesus assured Peter that he would return to a place of strength and would bring encouragement to the brethren.

Several years ago, I experienced a time of intense sifting. I have never felt such brokenness and despair in my life. God brought me through that season of sifting to restoration. I have now returned to encourage the brethren.

May you be encouraged as you read the pages of this book.

Grace and Peace in His Name

Dr. Daryl G. Donovan

Table Of Contents

CHAPTER 1

The Wilderness Testimony

When once you have turned again, strengthen the brothers.

— Luke 22:32

God called me to preach when I was seventeen. I loved Jesus and the Word of God and wanted to share His Good News. After completing high school, I went off to college preparing for ministry. Little did I know that my real preparation for ministry would take place fifteen years later in a Texas wilderness alone with God

For fifteen years I struggled in ministry, striving to do the things of God in my own strength. At the age of 32 I was broken and burned out. I had been working on my Doctorate of Ministry while pastoring full time. I had no personal devotional life — no prayer time — no regular time to meditate upon the Word of God. Because of my failure to enrich my relationship with Jesus, I became physically exhausted and spiritually bankrupt. In deep despair, I found myself enslaved to various hideous sins. To put it simply: my life was a mess.

Probably only the Lord and I knew just how bad things were. To some extent I could hide my problems from my congregation. In the midst of this hopeless despair I sensed the Spirit of the Lord say to me, "Lay it all down. Come away and spend time at My feet." At the time I wasn't sure what "lay it all down" meant, but in the days to come God made that very clear to me.

I discerned from the Lord that I must resign my pastorate, stop work on my doctorate, sell my possessions and go to the wilderness. I felt much like God was my Master Coach, pulling me out of the game for a while to sit on the bench until I learned to listen to Him. While "forsaking all" was very painful, because I knew it was His will, I had the courage to go through with it.

I remember the night I resigned from my church. When I announced that I must leave, one of the elders, a faithful man of prayer, immediately said, "Let's pray." After a few moments of silent prayer that same elder said, "We need to support Daryl in this decision." The group agreed and pledged prayerful support.

It may seem odd, but I remained, serving the congregation sixty days following the resignation, fulfilling my contract. During those two months God worked in our fellowship in miraculous ways. We saw many come to know Jesus as Savior and Lord. The whole church experienced a fresh outpouring of the Holy Spirit. While it was difficult for some to understand why I had to leave, it was clear to most, that it was God's will.

At the end of December, 1985, I drove away from that great congregation with all that I owned in the back seat of my little, worn-out Honda Civic. I didn't know where I was going, nor what I was going to do. It was clear I was to do my best to hear God and that He would lead the way.

I ended up spending about three weeks on my parents' abandoned farm place. I slept on the floor of the empty house, spending my days helping Dad remodel the house, preparing it for sale. My dad was terrific during those days. While he said he didn't understand, he was very loving and supportive. God used those three weeks as a beautiful bonding time between Dad and me.

In the bleak cold of January, 1986, it was time to load up my car again. Led by the Spirit to go down to the wilderness, I simply started driving south. I drove as far south as Houston, Texas, stopping there to seek the Lord for further instructions. As I opened the road map my eyes fell immediately upon the word, "Victoria." Victoria, Texas, would be my place of victory. God was leading me to this Texas wilderness to allow Him to do a mighty work of restoration.

When I arrived in Victoria, I didn't know where to go or what God wanted me to do next, so I checked into a motel. The entire night was spent seeking my Heavenly Father for guidance. That night I clearly sensed the Spirit of the Lord giving me the following instructions:

1. I was to anoint myself with oil, pouring the entire bottle over my head.
2. I was to bathe myself "as a newborn babe."
3. I was prompted to begin a fast that would last forty days and nights. (I was to eat only fruits and vegetables in small portions.)
4. No razor was to touch my head.

5. The Bible would be my constant companion during this time, and I was prompted by the Spirit to read it carefully from cover to cover.

The next morning I found a room in a boarding house outside of Victoria. I got a job at McDonald's (try that while fasting) so that I would have enough money to pay the landlady. I did as God directed and in the next forty days God did His wonderful work of making a new man.

During the forty-day fast, I read extensively in the Bible daily. I meditated upon it. I sensed God cleansing and renewing me. Even though I had been to both college and seminary, I was reading much of the Bible for the first time.

Near the end of the forty days an angel appeared to me in a dream telling me only this, "Arise and return." The next night, he appeared again giving the same directive, "Arise and return." On the third consecutive night, the angel appeared and said, "Have I not now told you this the third time to arise and return?" As the angel spoke those words, I awoke. I was sobbing.

I told God that I wasn't sure if I was ready to return. I did not want to go through such pain ever again — nor put people I loved through such anguish. I said, "God, I don't want to ever fall like this again!" He gently spoke to my spirit and said, "You do not have to. I will teach you how to stand." I reached for my Bible and was led to 2 Peter, chapter one. God's Spirit spoke and said, "It's all there."

I began to read the words penned by a man who had fallen. Peter had been a broken man who had been "sifted like wheat" (Luke 22:31), but he had returned. Now with new confidence, Peter was writing words to "encourage the brethren" (Luke 22:31). When I read the words, "as long as you practice these things you will never stumble," the tears began to flow again. God had brought me to this place to restore me and now He was showing me the way to prevent ever falling again.

I did arise and return. I drove as far as Arkansas, staying with Christian friends there. While sitting on the edge of a cliff one day I heard a voice behind me say, "They will come seeking you."

12

That night an elder called from the congregation from which I had resigned. They wanted me to come back.

The next week I returned to meet with the elders. An elder's wife pulled me aside and said, "Daryl, there is something I must ask you. Buck (another of the elders) says that an angel has come to you four times to encourage you to come back. Is that true?" I couldn't speak. I began to sob. Almost as both a statement and question she said to me, "Then it is true." Through tears I muttered, "Yes." God was bringing me back as a new man to encourage the brethren.

I am writing this book because I must! God has so graciously put me back on my feet and I know He wants to do the same for others. I had bought the lie that the Christian faith was just a series of ups and downs. I thought it "normal" that we would spend a good deal of our time fumbling and stumbling around, pulling ourselves up again and again. I now know that God wants us to enjoy consistent victorious stability. He said, "As long as you practice these things you will never stumble" (2 Peter 1:10).

Please prayerfully read the following pages allowing God to make your footsteps sure. Let the Holy Spirit restore and establish you. Learn to stand — and walk in Him without stumbling.

Questions For Discussion

1. Respond to Dr. Donovan's testimony:

2. Do you think it is possible to learn how to walk without stumbling in the spiritual life?

3. Could you share a testimony with the group about an area of your own life that you thought impossible to change, but God helped you to do so?

CHAPTER 2

Learning To Walk

. . . as long as you practice these things, you will never stumble.

— 2 Peter 1:11 (N.A.S.)

As we packed up our gear and headed for the snow-covered slopes of the Colorado Rockies, my heart pounded with anticipation and anxiety (not to mention terror). I was embarking upon my first attempt at snow skiing. Here I was, 37 years old and, up to this point, wise enough to stay on sure footing. But I let our youth group coerce me into this adventure.

I will never forget the thoughts I had as the ski lift approached for me to "hop on." I felt certain that I would either break my neck — or break the neck of the person I would plow into. When we arrived at the top of the bunny slope, I gracefully tumbled off of the lift. My instructor only rolled his eyes. Somehow I made it down the face of that mountain. In fact, by afternoon after several runs, I was having a good time. I had learned to ski . . . at least a little.

Honestly, I went to those slopes with very low expectations of ever learning to ski. I fully anticipated countless tumbles down the mountain, with the final conclusion being a lengthy vacation in the hospital.

I had accomplished what I had earlier thought to be impossible. I had learned to ski without stumbling and bumbling down the mountain out of control. I was able to exercise control — ensuring a safe, enjoyable adventure down the snow-packed slope.

My skiing experience illustrates what can happen for each of us in the spiritual realm as we commit our lives to the Lord Jesus Christ. Under the guidance and empowerment of our great Instructor, the Holy Spirit, we can be enabled to travel the Christian adventure with stability, security and delight.

Unfortunately, my own experience, and what I observe in the lives of others, has convinced me that most Christians continue to stumble and tumble, failing to learn to walk in consistent victory. For most of my life as a Christian, I regularly fell prey to temptation and sin. I was undisciplined — uncontrolled and unfruitful. My walk with Christ was marked almost daily by a series of stumbles and falls. It seemed I could never learn how to walk the Christian walk.

It took a hard fall for me to finally wake up to the truth that God had something better in mind for me. He showed me how to begin to stand firm . . . to walk secure.

In the next several weeks, as we share in this study together, I believe God is going to help you learn to walk out your Christian faith in stability and victory you once thought to be unobtainable. By God's grace, you can learn to walk without stumbling! Isn't that exciting?

As I shared in chapter one, God taught me how to walk through the words of the Apostle Peter. This passage found in 2 Peter, chapter 1, will be the framework for our study. Let's read it together.

2. Grace and peace be multiplied to you in the knowledge of God and of Jesus our Lord;
3. Seeing that his divine power has granted to us everything pertaining to life and godliness, through the true knowledge of Him who called us by His own glory and excellence.
4. For by these He has granted to us His precious and magnificent promises, in order that by them you might become partakers of the divine nature, having escaped the corruption that is in the world by lust.
5. Now for this very reason also, applying all diligence, in your faith supply moral excellence, and in your moral excellence, knowledge;
6. And in your knowledge, self-control, and in your self-control, perseverance, and in your perseverance, godliness;
7. And in your godliness, brotherly kindness, and in your brotherly kindness, love.
8. For if these qualities are yours and are increasing, they render you neither useless nor unfruitful in the true knowledge of our Lord Jesus Christ.

9. For he who lacks these qualities is blind or short-sighted, having forgotten his purification from his former sins.

10. Therefore, brethren, be all the more diligent to make certain about His calling and choosing you; for as long as you practice these things, you will never stumble;

11. For in this way the entrance into the eternal kingdom of our Lord and Savior Jesus Christ will be abundantly supplied to you.

— 2 Peter 1:2-11

Did you notice the last part of verse 10? "... as long as you practice these things, you will never stumble." Yes, it says never stumble. Isn't that great news!

Why do some miss learning how to walk without stumbling? Let me share a few possible reasons we are delayed in learning how to walk.

First of all, I think some people experience a "stumbling" walk with Jesus just because they don't know any better. For many years, I thought that it was just the nature of the Christian life to be falling and getting up again. Other believers told me often, "We all stumble." Therefore, I just lived out what I thought to be the norm.

There is far too much ignorance in the Body of Christ today as to the promises and provisions of God to enable us to stand — and walk in triumph. Many have bought the lies, "I can't change," "I'm only human," or "We all fall," rather than hearing and receiving the truth that we can walk without falling.

The second reason many Christians continue to tumble is lack of discipline. I had come to the point that I knew God wanted better for me, but I refused to exercise the proper discipline to obtain it. It is a bit like the ski slope story. Sometime during my first run down the hill it dawned on me, "I can do this!" It took commitment, hard work and discipline to get to the place where I could ski with some confidence and stability.

Discipline is not a pleasant word for some. Too often we want to achieve instant spiritual maturity, with as little effort on our part as possible. We want God to operate as some "fast food" restaurant, filling us up quickly, making us into spiritual giants. In a society that offers instant breakfast, wealth, sexual gratification, divorce, and so forth, we want instant spiritual maturity as well.

Many times during my fumbling, stumbling years, I prayed asking God to bring stability to my life. I prayed for guidance — but never took time to listen for His response. I begged for wisdom and knowledge, yet spent little time reading the Bible to obtain it. I cried out for victory over temptation, but rarely turned to Him for the means of escape when it came. Due to my lack of discipline, my Christian life remained at best a crawl rather than a triumphant walk.

A third prohibition to a victorious walk is a failure to surrender to the Lordship of Jesus Christ and to the guidance of the Holy Spirit. My life consisted of the typical battle between the Spirit and the flesh, with the flesh winning most of the time. Sin was still calling the shots. Although we may have the knowledge of God's provision for our walk and we may apply hearty discipline with that knowledge, if we have not totally surrendered, we will not enjoy the walk He has in store for us.

Sin-free Living?

About now, you may be scratching your head and saying, "Does he mean I can live the Christian life without ever sinning?" That's a fair question. Let me try to answer it.

I believe that we who belong to Christ are no longer slaves to sin. As the Apostle Paul wrote:

> *Therefore we have been buried with Him through baptism into death in order that as Christ was raised from the dead through the glory of the Father, so we too might walk in newness of life.*
> *For if we have become united with Him in the likeness of His death, certainly we shall be also in the likeness of His resurrection.*
> *Knowing this, that our old self was crucified with Him, that our body of sin might be done away with, that we should no longer be slaves to sin.*
> *For he who has died is freed from sin.*
> — Romans 6:4-7

We are free from sin. Our lives are no longer governed by sin, nor are they characterized by persistent fumbles and stumbles. We have been empowered to walk in a new way.

That does not mean, however, that we have obtained spiritual perfection. Paul said it well in Philippians 3:12: "Not that I have already become perfect, but I press on in order that I may lay hold of that for which also I was laid hold of by Christ Jesus." While we have learned to walk without stumbling, we are still pressing on, being conformed to the image of Jesus (Romans 8:29), being transformed by the renewing of our minds (Romans 12:2).

Let me illustrate what I mean. When I was eleven months old I was a stumbler. No one would have gazed upon that precious, little, red-headed baby and said, "Oh look, doesn't he walk well!" While I don't remember all the bumps and bruises, reliable sources have assured me that I experienced many painful tumbles before I became a "walker."

The great day did arrive when I began to walk. I still swayed a bit, but everyone knew my crawling days were behind me. My walking skills improved day by day. Soon I was no longer a stumbler. I had become a confident walker.

A few weeks ago while rushing into Wal-Mart, I slipped on a slick spot in the parking lot. Wow! Did I take a tumble. Fortunately, my pride was bruised more than my body. Because I took that fall, did that mean I was not a walker anymore? Would I be labeled a stumbler? Because it is not normal that I fall down every time I go to Wal-Mart (thank goodness), I am still considered as one who walks well.

My point is this. In the spiritual realm are you a stumbler or a walker? What typifies your walk with Jesus? For me, most of my Christian life consisted of falls and tumbles. For many years I did not achieve any measure of consistent stability in my spiritual life. That is where too many Christians are today . . . continuing to stumble.

While we will have times when we slip and fall, those times should be the exception, not the rule. It must be our goal to press on to the biblical standard to walk without stumbling.

Why is this so important?

There are several reasons it is crucial for Christians to hear the call to walk tall!

I. It is God's will!

He would not have told us how to walk without stumbling if we could not do so. "As long as you practice these things you will never stumble" (2 Peter 1:10). He would not have said that Jesus is able to keep us from stumbling if that were not the truth. "Now to Him who is able to keep you from stumbling, and to make you stand in the presence of His glory blameless with great joy" (Jude v. 24).

II. We will enjoy life more!

Falling is no fun. You always get a bump or two — sometimes you even break things. The more we walk in consistent victory with Him, the more we enjoy His peace. That does not mean pain free living — but at least it isn't self-inflicted any more by our refusal to learn how to walk.

III. A Walking witness wins the world!

When I was stumbling around, falling often into temptation and sin, I wondered why I couldn't lead a lot of people to Christ. It was because they saw nothing different in my life. I worried as much as they did. I told the same stories, went to the same movies and got just as depressed. I looked no different than a lost person. No light was shining. You cannot pick up another as long as you are still falling.

IV. There's a rough road ahead!

We have got to learn to walk now, for in the days ahead the road will only get more treacherous. I am no prophet, but I believe we could be approaching the last days. Whether that be the case or not, it is obviously true that it is getting more difficult each day for the Christian to stand firm and walk in consistent victory. Temptations abound. There was a time when peer pressure encouraged good behavior. Now, sin is glorified. Morality has been painted as gray rather than black or white, with no absolute right or wrong. The pressure is intensified; the road much rougher, laden with explosive mines. We must learn to walk now. We must walk with skill and alertness, led and empowered by the Holy Spirit.

21

Questions For Discussion

1. How would you define spiritually walking without stumbling?

2. Would you consider yourself a stumbler or a walker?

3. Are you a disciplined Christian? Why or why not?

4. Why is it so important that we learn how to walk without stumbling?

5. Is there an area in your life in which you would like to achieve consistent victory and thus far you have been unable to do so? Can you talk about it with the group?

6. Are you committed to being able to walk without stumbling?

CHAPTER 3

Faith Is The Starting Point

. . . applying all diligence in your faith . . . .

— 2 Peter 1:5

The Apostle Peter understood that the place to begin when seeking to stand was faith. Every other pointer Peter presents is precluded by faith. If we fail to comprehend the importance of faith, we will fail to stand.

What is faith? Let's look first at what it is not. First of all, faith is not a mere mental concession in which we utter words expressing our belief. When one says, "I believe God will provide," yet he wrings his hands fretting when and how He will do it, are his words a display of faith? If a person correctly and concisely recites a confession of faith saying, "I believe that Jesus is the Christ, the Son of the living God and I accept Him as my personal Lord and Savior," yet continues to hope he is good enough to escape Hell... is that person exemplifying faith?

Many live a life marked by stumbling because they understand faith to be a matter of "believing" the right things and saying the right words. Faith is much more.

Secondly, faith is not something we produce to get God to do what we want. There are those who seem to think that health, wealth and prosperity are ours for the claiming (if we just have enough faith). The image comes to my mind of God as some supernatural "bellhop" who must respond to our bidding when we ring the bell of faith.

How many saints have stumbled because their false understanding of faith has prompted them to believe they are "faith failures" — or that God has failed them by not responding appropriately? Because some have put their faith in their faith, they have failed to stand.

So what is Faith?

Let me share with you a simple, Biblical definition of faith. Faith is hearing God and responding accordingly. Paul said to the Romans, "So faith comes from hearing, and hearing by the Word of Christ" (Romans 10:17). Faith is conceived in our hearts as we hear God speak. It is perfected, or completed, as we respond. James wrote, "Was not Abraham our father justified by works, when he offered up Isaac his son on the altar? You see that faith was working with his works, and as a result of the works, faith was perfected" (James 2:21-22). He went on to write in Chapter 2, verse 26, "For just as the body without the Spirit is dead, so also faith without works is dead."

Abraham heard God say what to do. "Take now your son, your only son, whom you love, Isaac, and go to the land of Moriah, and offer him there as a burnt offering on one of the mountains of which I will tell you" (Genesis 22:2). Would Abraham have been considered the great man of faith if he had said, "I hear you God," but then took Isaac fishing instead? His faith was perfected in his willingness to obey—to respond accordingly to God's directive.

Have you read the great "faith chapter" in Hebrews 11? (Take time to do so now.) The Author says that faith is the assurance of things hoped for, the conviction of things not seen. The Greek root word for assurance literally means nature or reality. Faith is something real and tangible.

The writer of Hebrews goes on to give numerous examples of real faith. Notice in each case: the person of faith heard God and responded accordingly. Noah heard God say, "Build," so he did. Abraham heard God say, "Go," so he went not knowing where he was going. Sarah and Abraham conceived Isaac by faith, which included an act of faith, for Isaac is never described as an immaculate conception.

The closing verses of Hebrews 11 describe those who were willing to sacrifice, suffer and even die responding in their faith. They had heard the Gospel and considered it worth dying for. Real faith always produces some genuine response or transformation.

Faith to stand . . .

How does our understanding of faith affect our ability to stand? We will stand and walk confidently as we strive to hear God and respond appropriately. If we continue to regard faith as merely believing or saying the right things, we will continue to stumble.

25

Let me give a few illustrations to clarify how faith works, enabling us to stand. Since I believe that God speaks most often and most clearly through the Bible, my examples will come from directives given there.

God speaks in Matthew 6:14-15: "For if you forgive men for their transgressions, your heavenly Father will also forgive you. But if you do not forgive men, then your Father will not forgive your transgressions." If someone were to say, "I believe that" . . . yet continued to hold a grudge, has that person exercised faith? It is one thing to consent to the Word of God, and another thing to commit to it. The liberating joy of experiencing God's forgiveness fully will not come until faith is fulfilled by forgiving first!

God speaks in Matthew 28:19: "Go therefore and make disciples of all the nations, baptizing them in the name of the Father and the Son and the Holy Spirit teaching them to observe all that I commanded you." I have not had one Christian profess disbelief that the great commission is a directive given to all God's people. Yet how many say they believe it but fail to respond? We miss the life-transforming blessing for ourselves in our unwillingness to share Christ and His teachings with others. Our own faith is unfulfilled because we have failed to respond to God's command.

God spoke through the Apostle Paul saying, "Abstain from every form of evil" (1 Thessalonians 5:22). We believe that we should abstain, yet we fail to respond accordingly. We seek to gratify our flesh, ignoring the consequences of sin clearly spelled out in God's Word, and we participate in many forms of evil. We forfeit countless blessings because our faith is not perfected.

Faith and obedience are inseparable. It is only in their union that we find real life. Obedience without faith is usually legalism— or self-righteousness. Faith without obedience is not really faith at all.

Have you ever wondered why nearly 90 percent of Americans profess faith in God, yet it is not evidenced in our society? It is because they say they believe, yet their hearts are far from God. There has not been a response of surrender and obedience to the Living Holy God. Ninety percent of Americans may express belief — but they do not express faith.

Is this Works Righteousness?

Before you tag me a "works righteousness" proponent, let me say that obedience is not the only appropriate response in the completion of real faith.

The great people of faith who were sawn in half (Hebrews 11:37) did not so much respond with an action as they did with an attitude. Their devotion and love for Christ was so real they willingly (even joyously) died for the sake of his name.

The prophet Habakkuk expressed real faith, not in an act, but in pure trust when he wrote:

> *Though the fig tree should not blossom, and there be no fruit on the vines, Though the yield of the olive shall fail, and the fields produce no food, Though the flock should be cut off from the fold, and there be no cattle in the stalls, Yet will I exult in the Lord. I will rejoice in the God of my salvation.*
> *The Lord God is my strength, and He has made my feet like Hinds feet, and makes me walk on many high places.*
> — Habakkuk 3:17-19

Real faith responds with constant trust, even when the cattle stalls or the kitchen cabinets are empty. Paul expressed his faith when he wrote, "I know how to get along with humble means, and I also know how to live in prosperity; in any and every circumstances I have learned the secret of being filled and going hungry; both of having abundance and suffering need" (Philippians 4:12).

The response of gratitude is a clear indication of perfected faith. It is apparent to me that the person who constantly grumbles, frets and walks in fear has not experienced the faith that will enable one to stand.

But what about mountain moving?

Faith is not only vital for our "every day" ability to stand and walk in victory, it is the key to experiencing the supernatural and miraculous. It is by faith that we see the lame walk, the blind see, the demons flee and the sea parted. By faith we walk in the power of God that is beyond ourselves — beyond this world. But the definition of faith is still the same. It is hearing God and responding accordingly.

The reason some mountains are not moved is because we did not hear God say they should be moved. We just thought they needed to be moved, so we tried to muster up enough faith to get them moved. We never considered that God might have those mountains there to teach us to climb!

The reason people aren't getting that Mercedes is not their lack of belief. It is because God has said a Ford will do. Or He might be saying walk. He might not even mention your mode of transportation at all.

The reason Joni Erickson Tada has not risen from her wheelchair is because God has said He can receive greater glory with her in that position rather than on her feet.

Consider carefully the miracles in Scripture. Either explicitly or implicitly God has spoken prior to the event in each case. God told Moses to lift up his rod and that He would part the Red Sea — it wasn't Moses' idea. God told Joshua how to defeat Jericho and Joshua responded accordingly . . . and won! Jesus told Peter to come to Him on the water — it was not merely on Peter's own initiative.

As we keep our ear tuned to the voice of the Great Shepherd and hear His commands, we will see similar miracles today. In a prayer service one evening a woman came to me and said, "I believe God just said that we are to lay hands on Mary and pray for her to be healed of her cancer and she will be." I consented to her request. After we prayed the same woman whispered, "Now you are to tell her that God has healed her." Reluctantly I said, "Mary, God said… (long pause)… you're going to be all right." She was all right. GOD DID HEAL HER! God had spoken and by His grace we had responded accordingly.

It is a time to be alert to God's voice. It is a time to be willing to respond when He speaks. Like Jesus, we should be about the business of what the Father is doing and saying (John 5:19 and 5:30). As we walk seeking to know God's heart, hearing His voice and responding accordingly, we will stand tall and walk in confidence.

Questions For Discussion

1. In this chapter, faith is defined as "hearing God speak and responding accordingly." Respond to that definition. Do you agree?

2. How does one's understanding of faith affect one's ability to stand? Can you see how a misunderstanding of faith can be a cause for stumbling? Discuss:

3. With the definition of faith that is given in this chapter, what is the key to experiencing miracles today?

4. Are there "faith areas" in your own life in which you have said, "I believe that," but you have not completed your faith with the appropriate response? Discuss:

5. Share faith encounters: instances in which you have heard God's clear directive, you responded accordingly and you saw God act. (Example: There was a man who heard God's directive on tithing, believed it, yet failed to do it for a number of years. One day he decided to respond accordingly . . . he began to tithe. Immediately his finances began to get in order.)

CHAPTER 4

Maintaining Moral Excellence

. . . applying all diligence, in your faith, supply moral excellence . . . .

— 2 Peter 1:15

After the Apostle Peter wrote that faith is the starting point for all of us to be able to walk, he admonished us to add goodness to our faith. The New American Standard translation calls it moral excellence. The second step in learning to walk stable and secure is moral excellence. We are encouraged to be men and women with the utmost of moral integrity.

Before you flex your muscles and determine that "you're gonna be good" from now on, let me remind you of a couple of important Biblical truths. First of all, goodness or moral excellence is a fruit of the Spirit. In Galatians chapter five we find the fruit of the Spirit-filled life:

> *But the fruit of the Spirit is love, joy, peace, patience, kindness, goodness, faithfulness, gentleness, self-control; against such things there is no law.*
>
> — Galatians 5:22-23

Goodness or moral excellence is not something you produce. It is something the Holy Spirit produces in you. It is a fruit of your relationship with the Father, as you are indwelled by His Spirit. I have seen so many Christians "try to be good." They work hard at doing the right thing or not doing the wrong thing. While I commend their desire to be disciplined, I grieve to see their misdirection in thinking they can achieve moral excellence by the work of the flesh.

The second truth is this: moral excellence is found in surrendering to the guiding, correcting work of the Holy Spirit. Let the Helper help you know what is right and wrong. It is His responsibility to convict of sin and to convince of righteousness (John 16:8-9). The Holy Spirit will lead you into moral excellence if you are willing to listen to him.

Here is an example of what I mean by allowing the Holy Spirit to lead you into moral excellence. As a pastor, I was deeply concerned with Christian young people's involvement with secular rock music. Some of it is blatantly demonic. As an outreach ministry, I began duplicating my Christian tapes and giving them to our youth. One day a college student said to me, "Don't you know that what you are doing is illegal?" I became defensive and explained to him that as long as I was not selling the tapes, what I was doing was fine. Besides, it was a ministry.

After my conversation with the college student, I did begin to feel some conviction about the tapes, so I prayed about it. I asked God to show me if I was in error. He did show me and I was in error. He gently led me to look at the label on the tapes I owned. It said: "*Any* unauthorized reproduction of this cassette is unlawful." It just said, "any." It did not say it was all right if I gave them away, or even if it were a part of my ministry.

I quit making illegal tapes because I was willing to let the Holy Spirit show me the truth. He gave me the provision to give the young people original albums, thereby benefiting the whole kingdom of God.

Don't forget these two principles as you move on to stand in moral excellence. One, the Holy Spirit produces moral excellence as a fruit in you. Two, you must be willing to listen to the Holy Spirit lead you in the path of righteousness.

A Clean Heart

David had committed an awful sin with Bathsheba. Not only that, he had Uriah, her husband, killed. David was sorry for his sin and he humbled himself before God and sought forgiveness. The important thing to notice about David is that he did not instantly make pledges to "do better next time." He did not call upon his human strength to overcome temptation so that he would not fall into this sin again. He began with his heart. Let's look at Psalm 51, penned shortly after David's sin was exposed.

> *1. Be Gracious to me, O God, according to Thy loving kindness;*
> *According to the greatness of Thy compassion blot out my transgressions.*

2. Wash me thoroughly from my iniquity, and cleanse me from my sin.

3. For I know my transgressions, and my sin is ever before me.

4. Against Thee, Thee only, I have sinned, and done what is evil in Thy sight,
So that Thou art justified when Thou dost speak,
And blameless when Thou dost judge.

5. Behold, I was brought forth in iniquity,
And in sin my mother conceived me.

6. Behold, Thou dost desire truth in the innermost being,
And in the hidden part Thou wilt make me know wisdom.

7. Purify me with hyssop, and I shall be clean;
Wash me, and I shall be whiter than snow.

8. Make me to hear joy and gladness, Let the bones which Thou hast broken rejoice.

9. Hide Thy face from my sins,
And blot out all my iniquities.

10. Create in me a clean heart, O God,
And renew a steadfast spirit within me.

11. Do not cast me away from Thy presence,
And do not take Thy Holy Spirit from me.

12. Restore to me the joy of Thy salvation,
And sustain me with a willing spirit.

— Psalms 51:1-12

David knew that the secret to moral excellence was a clean heart. He knew he could not get back on track and walk in moral integrity unless God did heart surgery. In both Psalm 26 and 139, David calls upon the Lord to search his heart of anything unpleasing to the Father. The heart is the place to start to begin to stand in moral excellence.

David's son Solomon learned from his dad about the importance of a clean heart. In Proverbs 4:23, Solomon admonishes his son to "guard his heart." The prophets knew that Israel's atrocious sins were a result of dirty hearts. Jeremiah knew Israel must have her heart cleansed before restoration could occur (Jeremiah 4:14). Jesus said, "Blessed are the pure in heart, for they shall see God" (Matthew 5:8).

Allow God to search and test your heart and see if there is any wicked way in you. Allow the blood of Jesus to cleanse you and create in you a right spirit. You will never discover "goodness" on the outside if you haven't allowed the Spirit of God to create it on the inside.

I struggled with a recurring sin in my life. Have you ever had one of those persistent sins that just keeps coming back? I went to several counselors. I prayed. I even considered exorcism. When I was almost to the point of giving up and coming to the conclusion that this sin would always nag me, I found help.

A bold Christian counselor told me that my problem was a divided heart (Psalm 86:11). He told me that I loved my sin more than I loved Jesus. Of course, I graciously told him that he was mistaken. He reminded me of the words of Jesus in John chapter 14. "If you love me you will obey my commandments" (John 14:15). He asked me if I understood my sin to be in conflict with the teachings of Jesus. I said that I did. He very simply asked me then if I loved Jesus enough to obey Him, or was I going to continue to submit to my sin.

As I went home alone that evening, I made one of the most difficult confessions before my Lord Jesus that I have ever made. Through tears I admitted to Jesus that I loved my sin more than Him. I confessed my divided heart that desired more to please self than to please Jesus. There was a breaking that took place after that confession that I cannot explain. It was as if my heart had broken open and Jesus poured his blood over my heart cleansing and healing me. The divided heart was gone. The sin was gone.

What I had tried to do for so long was to conquer my sin in my own strength. I simply tried to change my outward actions, while my heart was still divided in its allegiance. It was no wonder I would stand for a while, but soon came crashing down. After my heart got right, the moral excellence began to flow.

Guard Your Mind

Directly related to our heart is our mind. We are encouraged in the Word to guard our hearts and minds. David asked the Lord to search his heart and mind. Evil deeds and words find their beginnings in the mind. Moral excellence cannot be discovered apart from a mind set upon pleasing God.

In 2 Corinthians 10:5 it says, "We are taking every thought captive to the obedience of Christ." We are not to just let evil thoughts run wild in our thinking. Be careful not to continually subject your mind to information contrary to the Kingdom of God.

I have observed so many Christians filling their minds with garbage. In one sense, we are like a fine computer: garbage in — garbage out. You cannot expect to have a mind set on pleasing God if you daily provide your thought processes with a steady diet of corruption.

In one pastorate I served I worked with a deacon who read his horoscope daily. I asked him if he believed in astrology. He said that he did not, but that he just read the horoscope for fun. During the time that I knew him, many times I heard him quote his horoscope when various circumstances would arise. His mind was tainted by an ungodly influence to which he had subjected himself.

A faithful lady was active in about every church function we had. The only time I noticed she did not attend was in the afternoon meetings. I asked one of the other women why "Beulah" never attended the afternoon meetings. The woman grinned and said, "Soaps." I knew exactly what she meant. For several hours every afternoon this Christian woman was filling her mind with scenes of adultery, murder, rape, homosexuality and profanity. This same "soap watching" woman spoke up in a meeting one time and said, "Many times divorce is the best option. If they'd both be happier with someone else, why not get a divorce?" She had received that teaching from her afternoon counselor. Moral excellence will never be found as long as we continue to subject our minds to moral degradation.

Many Christians today enjoy watching horror movies. I know some Christians who have seen all of the *Friday the 13th* movies and know more about Freddie from Elm Street than they do about some of their family members. I was a Christian who spent far too much time opening my mind to perversion, demonism, butchery and other horrid acts of violence. God showed me His desire for my mind and I set a guard as to what would enter. I realized that I was not going to be able to walk in victory unless I was willing to guard my mind. Be careful what you read, watch and hear.

Set Your Mind

Part of guarding your mind is setting it on the "right stuff." Paul in his epistle to the Philippians encourages them… and us… to set our minds on the good.

Finally, brethren, whatever is true, whatever is honorable, whatever is right, whatever is pure, whatever is lovely, whatever is of good repute, if there is any excellence, and if anything worthy of praise, let your mind dwell on these things.

— Philippians 4:8

If you will determine to set your mind on the things of God, you will see a remarkable difference in your life. Your attitude will become more positive. You will find the joy Jesus came to give you. The peace that passes all understanding will come. Rather than having a mind that dwells on the morbid, perverse, obscene, violent or ungodly, you've got a mind set on God.

The television doesn't blare unrestricted in our home. We carefully monitor all secular programs. Most of the time we watch family films or Christian videos. I listen only to Christian recording artists now. I find that both the words and the music edify and bring glory to my Father. I am also very select in what I read. While I do read enough secular material to keep up on current events, I spend most of my time reading the Bible and a few excellent Christian periodicals. It has been said that you are what you read. With the massive amounts of pornographic literature being consumed in this nation, is it any wonder we are becoming a society bent on sexual gratification and perversion?

I have made a conscious decision to set my mind on more lovely things and I have discovered the Holy Spirit renewing my mind. I have been accused of being narrow-minded. I simply choose to set my mind on what promotes the principles of the Kingdom of God. I do not choose to allow my mind to be a funnel (or perhaps gutter is a better word), receiving every bit of information the world has to offer.

Christian, guard your mind and set it on the things of God. Moral excellence, which is a giant step toward walking in triumph, can only be achieved when we allow the Holy Spirit to renew our minds, and that renewing is enhanced when we decide that the garbage doesn't funnel there anymore.

So What About our Actions?

Our heart is clean, check? Check! Our mind is being renewed and set on God, check? Check! Now we are ready to move on to moral excellence in our actions. If your heart and mind were not right you could do a lot of right things, but your motives would be impure. Furthermore, without a clean heart and sound mind you will never consistently achieve correct moral actions. With the foundation of a pure heart and a set mind, it is time to do the will of the Father. Moral-excellent actions involve both what we should not do and what we should be doing as those who belong to Him.

Some of This Has Got to Stop!

You are probably involved in some actions that are harmful to you and to those around you. You have heard the gentle tug of the Holy Spirit telling you that whatever you are doing needs to stop. Now is the time to plug in to the power of God and lay it down.

Decide it will cease today! One woman I knew was a compulsive gossip. (Men gossip, too. This just happens to be about a woman.) Her vicious tongue was hurting so many people. I visited with her extensively about this sin. She said that she knew it was sin and that she knew that God was not pleased with her actions. She just did not believe she could stop. We talked about her heart. We reflected upon what was filtering into her mind. She seemed to understand, yet nothing was changing. Finally one day she decided to correct her behavior. She determined to no longer be a gossip. God met her with grace and strength . . . and she overcame her sin.

I have met Christians who seem to desire some "magic fairy dust" to just fall upon them so they will instantly overcome some sinful habit. One "smoker" friend of mine said that he figured that when and if God wanted him to stop smoking that God would make cigarettes taste bad to him. God *might* do it that way.

Ordinarily, God is looking for an obedient heart and a willing spirit to carry out what the Spirit has been prompting. Finally, you must decide to obey!

We have responsibility in our victory over sin. We must decide to repent — turn away from that sin. We must flee temptation! Jesus told the woman who had been caught in adultery to "go and sin no more!" Decide today to "lay aside every encumbrance, and the sin which so easily entangles us, and let us run with endurance the race set before us" (Hebrews 12:1).

Don't Grow Weary in Doing Good

And let us not lose heart in doing good, for in due time we shall reap if we do not grow weary. So then, while we have opportunity, let us do good to all men, and especially to those who are of the household of faith.
— Galatians 6:9-10

Doing good is a delight! Not only that, it carries with it blessing and promise. We shall reap joy, friendships, a clear conscience, and most of all the knowledge that you have assisted others in seeing God. Moral excellence comes not only from avoiding evil, but in joyfully doing good!

Every day look for opportunities to do good. You will find even greater pleasure in your doing good if you do it anonymously without recognition. Your Heavenly Father knows. Help the needy; feed the poor; clothe the naked; listen to the hurting. Go get groceries for that shut-in. Babysit for that young couple so they can have a night out. Look for opportunities to do good!

A Fun Plan for Growing in Goodness

Several years ago God challenged me to do good whether anyone noticed or not. After all, the real integrity of a man is measured in secret. He also asked me if I could do a good deed and not tell one single person that I had done it. I said, "Sure!" Have you ever tried to do a good deed and not tell *anyone*? It isn't easy, but it surely is fun.

39

Let me give you a couple of suggestions:

Do you know someone in a financial dilemma? Send them some money anonymously. Remember, don't tell *anyone* that you did it. You will nearly split at your emotional seams, but you can do it. This is a good opportunity to check your motives.

I knew a man who made it a common practice to pay the toll for his car and the car behind him on the turnpikes. I'm sure folks in the car behind were thinking, "Who was that man?" Isn't this fun?

A friend of mine paid for the meal of the family behind him at McDonald's. They were total strangers. They never knew who blessed them. If you fill your days with "fun" ways of unselfishly doing good, you will find yourself walking in joy.

Let me caution you. Notice, the Turnpike Giver and the McDonald's Mystery Man didn't keep it a secret or I wouldn't know about it. Stretch yourself and keep your good deeds a secret.

Moral excellence fosters more moral excellence! It is a victorious cycle. Many stumble because they fail to make moral excellence a goal. Let this be the hour that you decide to walk with a clean heart, a mind set on God, and moral integrity that leads to joy.

Questions For Discussion

1. How do you achieve a clean heart?

2. What are some bad influences to which we subject our minds?

3. What immoral action have you seen put behind you in your life?

4. Is there some sin today that you would like the group to help you conquer?

5. List several "secret" good deeds you could do.

6. What other good behavior does God desire of us?

7. Have you made moral excellence your goal?

CHAPTER 5

It Is *What* You Know . . .
And *Who* You Know

. . . applying all diligence, in your faith . . . supply knowledge . . .

— 2 Peter 1:5

Having reminded us to be people of faith, supplying moral excellence to our walk in Christ Jesus, Peter then encourages us to supply knowledge. Lack of knowledge or ignorance is often a source of stumbling and Peter is giving us spiritual principles in order that we might never fall. In 2 Peter 1:3, Peter reminds us that the true *knowledge* of Him and of His divine power reveals to us that everything pertaining to life and godliness has been granted to us. When we walk in ignorance of who God is and of what He has accomplished for us through Jesus Christ, we are prone to stumble and fall.

There are several instances in scripture when ignorance led to stumbling. Paul said to the Church at Corinth, "I would not have you ignorant concerning spiritual gifts" (1 Corinthians 12:1). Because of lack of knowledge about the gifts of the Holy Spirit the Corinthian Church had fallen into misuse and abuse of the gifts.

In Acts, chapter 19, we find the Apostle Paul encountering some believers who were completely ignorant of the Holy Spirit. Paul said, "Did you receive the Holy Spirit when you believed?" They answered, "No, we have not even heard whether there is a Holy Spirit" (v. 2). These twelve men were ignorant of the full knowledge of God's divine power and were therefore not walking in the power of the Holy Spirit.

There was a greater ignorance that preceded the outpouring of the Holy Spirit upon the Church. Those who crucified Jesus were ignorant of what they were doing. Jesus said, "Father forgive them, for they *know not* what they are doing" (Luke 23:34). As they drove the nails, hurled abusive words and spat upon Jesus, it is quite clear they were unaware of who He was and what they were doing. They did not realize that this itinerant young preacher and healer was the only begotten Son of God.

Peter is calling us to be full of the knowledge of Jesus Christ. Many stumble trying to earn God's favor because they do not fully

44

comprehend what was accomplished at Calvary. There are those who say that Jesus was just a great teacher, not a Savior, and that we are to simply pattern our lives to His. They fall when they realize they cannot be like Jesus in their own strength.

In recent years, some liberal theologians have been teaching that Jesus was not *the* Christ, but a Christ. They hold that Buddah, Ghandi and others are also Christs. In their ignorance, they deny the atoning work accomplished only through Jesus Christ. Their ignorance will lead to a great stumbling!

In this chapter we are going to consider just what it is that Peter wants us to know. How do we realize the full and true knowledge of God and our Lord Jesus Christ? How will knowledge enable us never to stumble? More importantly, we will see that it is not just a matter of *what* you know, but *Who* you know.

Knowing God

What is eternal life? Would you say that eternal life is living forever? Perhaps you might say that it is going to Heaven. What did Jesus say eternal life is? Let's look at John 17:3: "And this is eternal life, that they *know* Thee the only true God, and Jesus Christ, whom Thou hast sent . . . ."

Eternal life is knowing God and Jesus Christ. It is not so much a quantity of life, but a quality of life: a life of knowing God. Eternal life is not something we must wait until after death to experience. It is a present reality of relationship with God through His Son Jesus Christ.

Peter understood that true knowledge begins with knowing Him. Abundant victorious life is found in knowing God. Peter knew that without the true knowledge of God and Jesus our Lord we could never walk secure. Our lives would be marred by constant stumbling. Knowing God ushers the believer into an eternal walk of stability and security.

Remember, however, that knowing God and knowing about God are not the same thing. Peter is not challenging us to merely learn all about God. He is calling us to know God. The word "know" denotes intimacy. Adam *knew* Eve and they bore a son. Joseph *knew* not Mary until Jesus was born. The kind of knowledge that will produce stability in the life of the believer is a relationship. It is knowing God intimately as Father and Friend. Peter had learned well from Jesus that eternal life was an intimate walk with God that sustains now and throughout eternity.

How do we know God?

God reveals Himself to us in many ways. We can get to know Him through several avenues. Here are a few Biblical suggestions for a starting place to discover a personal walk with God.

1. Nature itself speaks of His character. "For since the creation of the world His invisible attributes, His eternal power and divine nature, have been clearly seen, being understood through what has been made, so that they are without excuse" (Romans1:20).

Paul reminds us that God's very creation speaks of how awesome He is. People are without excuse who say there is no God. Look around you. Drink deeply of the beauty of God's creation and you will begin to see His power!

2. The Bible gives us a clear picture of God. READ ALL OF ISAIAH 40.

Isaiah understood the awesome power of God as well as God's tenderness to forgive and be a Shepherd. The Bible is full of reflections of God. We come to know Him through these Biblical pictures as we discover what He is like.

Not only do we see images of God in the Bible, but we hear Him speak. The Bible is like a divine love letter sent to planet earth from our Heavenly Father so that we might know Him.

I knew a couple who met on a train as the young man was leaving for Europe to fight in World War II. They exchanged addresses there on the train and wrote to each other throughout the war. They were married a few weeks after the young man's return from Europe. An intimate relationship had grown through their letter writing. We too can build an intimate relationship with God as we read His letter of love and revelation.

3. God has revealed Himself in Jesus Christ.

"God, after He spoke long ago to the fathers in the prophets in many portions and in many ways, in these last days has spoken to us in His Son, whom He appointed heir of all things, through whom also He made the world. And He is the radiance of His glory and the exact representation of His nature, and upholds all things by the word of His power" (Hebrews 1:1-3a).

To truly know God, we must know His Son. In John 10:30 Jesus said, "I and the Father are One." Through reading the Gospels, watching and listening to Jesus minister, you are able to observe what God is like. To fully experience the revelation of God the Father in the Son, let me encourage you to get a red-letter edition of the Bible. Go through the gospels and read only the red. You are reading all the recorded words of Jesus. You will hear the voice of the Father beckoning you to know Him.

Jesus is not merely a picture of the Father for us to know Him. Jesus is the Way to the Father. He is the bridge that spans the gap that sin has created between us and God. Jesus is the one who reconciles us to the Father through the cross (Colossians 1:19-20). According to Hebrews, Jesus is our great High Priest who was the once and for all sacrifice enabling us to enter the Holy of Holies to have intimate fellowship with God (Hebrews 7:25-27).

4. The Holy Spirit reveals the Father to us. "But when He, the Spirit of truth, comes, He will guide you into all truth; for He will not speak on His own initiative, but whatever He hears, He will speak; and He will disclose to you what is to come" (John 16:13).

The Holy Spirit is our Helper, Teacher and Counselor. He will lead us into all truth. He will reveal to us the full knowledge of God as we open ourselves to His divine indwelling. Ask to be filled with the Holy Spirit. Ask the Holy Spirit to show you who you are in Christ Jesus.

One night as I was reading the Bible, I came to some verses that brought tears to my eyes. The following passage of scripture reveals the depth of relationships possible:

For all who are being led by the Spirit of God, these are sons of God. For you have not received a spirit of slavery leading to fear again, but you have received a spirit of adoption as sons by which we cry out. "Abba! Father!"

— Romans 8:14-17

That word "Abba" means "daddy." It speaks of intimacy. The Holy Spirit reminds us that we are children of God. We are not slaves cowering in fear, but sons and daughters, joint heirs with Christ.

5. Prayer is a key to knowing God. "Devote yourselves to prayer, keeping alert in it with an attitude of thanksgiving" (Colossians 4:2).

Prayer keeps us alert in our relationship with God. It keeps an attitude of thanksgiving in our hearts. Prayer is intimate communion with the Father when we talk and when we listen.

If I were to say to you, "I'd like to get to know you," what would you think I meant? You would probably think I wanted to spend time with you and perhaps that I would want to share communication with you. When we say we want to get to know God it must mean we will spend quality time with Him. We will communicate with God. We will talk, laying bare our hearts, and we will listen, being still and knowing that He is God.

God desires for you to know Him. Remember He tore the veil of the temple in two from top to bottom symbolically saying, "Come in to the Holy of Holies." He wants to share a tender relationship with you and you will find that knowing Him will cause you to walk and never stumble.

Knowing God was paramount in Peter's mind as he called us to a knowledge that will produce stability. From our knowing God, there is more knowledge that comes to us enabling us to walk in confidence. We can know His promises and we can know His will.

Standing on the Promises

Many Christians stumble because they are ignorant of all of the promises available to them. We don't know or we forget who we are in Jesus Christ. There is a great storehouse of promises open to the believer. We cannot stand on promises we do not know. Let me remind you of just a few of the promises of God that help you to walk confidently.

1. You are loved. That seems simple to know but many of us have trouble receiving God's love. We feel unworthy or inadequate to be loved by God. When we hear that "God so loved the world," we forget that the world includes *us*! Romans 5:8 says that "God demonstrates His own love toward us, in that while we were yet sinners, Christ died for us." He did not wait until we got our act together to love us. He did not die for worthy people. He died for sinners. That is the kind of love He has for you and me. You are loved!

2. You are forgiven. If you have confessed your sin and sought God's forgiveness, you are forgiven. According to 1 John 1:9, when God forgives, He also cleanses us of all unrighteousness. It is behind us! That sin is no longer held in account against us (Psalm 10:10-12). I have seen Christians clinging to guilt over sins that God had forgiven and considered settled long ago.

Late for a meeting one night, I began my remarks with an apology for being late. In the introduction I apologized again. While sharing the first point, once again I apologized for being late. At my third apology, a woman piped up from the back and said, "You were forgiven the first time if you'd only received it."

Receive God's forgiveness today and know that you are cleansed from all unrighteousness.

3. You are empowered. Jesus sent to us a Helper. We cannot be the Church on our own. The Holy Spirit came to empower us to be witnesses. He brings gifts to us to minister and bring glory to Jesus Christ. When we try to walk out the Christian walk in the power of our own strength we are destined to fall.

There are so many promises. The promise that death does not have the final victory will enable us to walk tall through the valley of the shadow of death. The promise that we will reign with Christ will cause us to hold our head up high even when we are downtrodden. The promise that Jesus is returning will stir hope and joy in our hears, making our footsteps sure. Stand on the promises of God today and you will not stumble.

49

(An excellent resource here is a little book called *The Promise Book* found at your local Christian bookstore.)

Knowing God's Will

Paul prays a prayer for the Church at Colossae that we all can use. It is a prayer that they would know God's will:

> *9. For this reason also, since the day we heard of it, we have not ceased to pray for you and to ask that you may be filled with the knowledge of His will in all spiritual wisdom and understanding.*
>
> *10. So that you may walk in a manner worthy of the Lord, to please Him in all respects, bearing fruit in every good work and increasing in the knowledge of God.*
>
> — Colossians 1:9-10

When you are filled with the knowledge of His will for you, you will walk in a new confidence. When you know what the Father desires for you, you will walk in a manner worthy of the Lord.

I want to stretch your thinking a bit! In Matthew 5:48, Jesus admonishes us to be perfect even as our Heavenly Father is perfect. Most of us either struggle with that verse or ignore it. We say, "No one is perfect!" or "Jesus was the only perfect person!" I think Jesus was talking about knowing God's will.

Behind the meaning of the word "perfect" is the word "purpose." Let me explain what I mean:

One time I needed a screwdriver to fix the kitchen faucet. Elaine went to the tool room to bring me one. She brought a flat, regular screwdriver. I needed a Phillips-head screwdriver. She graciously made another trip and brought me the right screwdriver. As I placed the screwdriver on the screw, I exclaimed, "That's perfect!" The Phillips-head screwdriver was rusty, bent and had splotches of green paint on it — but it was perfect. Why? Because it was fulfilling the purpose for which it was designed.

You were designed for a purpose. Even though you may have flaws and weaknesses, you can walk in confident perfection. God has a perfect plan for you in His perfect will and when you discover His will, you will walk in new victory. Do you see why it is so important that we know God's will?

50

How do we know God's will for our lives? Let me give you five quick tips:

1. Abide in His Word, the Bible. Directives from others must not contradict God's Word.

2. Focus on the teachings and ministry of Jesus. Be a disciple. Follow His commands and example.

3. Listen to the leading of the Holy Spirit. That means keeping alert to His voice.

4. Spend quality quiet time in prayer. Jesus began each day in solitude with the Father.

5. Seek the counsel of a Godly advisor. God gives pastors, teachers and Christian friends to help us discover His will.

While God does not relay His will to us on a FAX machine, I do believe He makes it far more evident than most realize.

You can walk without stumbling. The Holy Spirit would not have had Peter write it if it were not true. The full knowledge of God and Jesus our Lord is a vital part of that secure, victorious walk. Get to know God, His promises, and His will, and you will walk!

Questions For Discussion

1. Do you feel like you know God?

2. What are the five Biblical principles for getting to know God? Can you think of other ways?

3. List ten (10) promises of God. Try to list others than those mentioned in the chapter.

4. Do you struggle with knowing God's will?

5. How can we better know His will for our lives?

6. Why is knowing God, His promises and His will so important to the Christian walk?

CHAPTER 6

Who's In Control

. . . applying all diligence in your faith, supply . . . self-control.

— 2 Peter 1:6

We have now discussed faith, moral excellence and knowledge. If we were to give careful attention to those three areas alone, I am sure we would find greater stability in our Christian walk. Peter, however, did not stop there. He encourages us to supply self-control.

Some of us cringe at the word self-control. We begin to think of bad habits that have plagued us for years. We are reminded of failures at discipline and self-control that have haunted us and brought discouragement. Fear not! Self-control does not totally depend upon you. Be encouraged! With the help of the Holy Spirit of God, you can become self-controlled.

As was true of moral excellence, self-control is a fruit of the Holy Spirit. That means that it is a by-product flowing from a relationship with the indwelling power of God's Spirit in our lives. Self-control is *not* merely your will to change. Self-control comes from your willingness to submit to the Spirit of God and allow Him to bring forth the change. You are involved in the process, as we will see, but the battle is not yours alone.

While we are not alone at developing self-control, we do have a significant responsibility. Even though the Bible is actually talking about the Spirit-controlled life when it mentions self-control, it is no accident that the word "self" precedes the word control instead of Spirit. Self is the human will. That human will must become submitted to the Holy Spirit to experience Godly self-control. Submission to the Holy Spirit is not a one-time event that is accomplished through one single act. When Jesus told us to take up our cross daily He knew that denial of the human will was a daily endeavor. Daily the self must be submitted to the Spirit's control. You must will daily, sometimes hourly, to allow God to direct. So you see, the main control is still in your hands. You will decide daily either to be led by the Spirit or by the flesh.

God will help you in submitting to the Holy Spirit. I am going to share with you some biblical principles for discovering Godly self-control. If you will apply these principles (that's your human will, too) you will find both your emotions and your actions coming under the harness of the Holy Spirit. You will walk in stability seeing an end to those outbursts of anger, fits of depression and bad habits that are destroying you.

But I'm Just Emotional

Lack of self-control reveals itself typically by emotional instability and habitual misbehavior. The Lord has impressed upon me that uncontrolled emotions cause far more Christians to stumble than do bad habits. In fact, many of those bad habits flow from emotional instability. Usually bad habits are only symptoms of a deeper spiritual/emotional problem. Emotions are harder to control. They are also easier to hide and deny, and are seated much closer to the very core of who we are than are bad habits or actions.

Do you explode with anger and then wonder why you got mad? Is jealousy a constant plague to your relationships with others? Do you consistently struggle with depression? Do you often feel inadequate and unloved? Having been hurt in the past, do you hold bitter grudges? These emotions can come under control. The Spirit of God will help you. You can walk in spiritual and emotional stability. Let me share with you ten scriptural guidelines for moving toward Spirit-controlled self-control.

Steps to Self-Control

1. Confess your sin. Admit before God specifically the areas of emotional instability that you know do not please Him. You may want to find a trusted Christian brother or sister and confess your struggle to that person as well (1 John 1:9, James 5:16).

2. Thank God for forgiving you and cleansing you of your sin. God is faithful. He has forgiven you. Thank Him for the blood of Jesus shed for you. Take time to reflect upon all that the cross means for you (1 John 1:9, Romans 5:1-8).

3. Repent of your sin. Turn away from your old emotional responses and move toward appropriate responses. A psychologist would tell you to change your patterns. Jesus told the adulteress to go and sin no more. Commit yourself to respond differently than

you normally do. If you are in the habit of cursing people who disturb you, bless them. If you tend to withdraw when you sense depression coming, force yourself to talk with someone. Repentance is not always an easy step, but it is always the right step (Acts 2:37).

4. Pray to be filled with the Holy Spirit. You may say, "But I am filled with the Holy Spirit!" We can experience fresh infilling daily. The Book of Acts is a record of many fillings of the Holy Spirit. We need to drink daily of the living waters God provides to sustain us (Ephesians 5:18).

5. Be clothed in Jesus. The Bible tells us to put on the Lord Jesus Christ. We are to daily be conformed to the image of Christ. Put on the whole armor of God, which is Jesus Christ, so that you can resist the Devil who taunts your emotions daily. Begin your day reading Colossians 3:12-17 or 1 Corinthians 13 (Ephesians 6:11, Galatians 3:27).

6. Screen what feeds your emotions. I am convinced that much of our emotional instability is a product of the media. Scenes of violence, revenge, hopelessness, perversion, and so forth, fill the television, radio and theater. A friend of mine watched the movie *The Exorcist* and was in a state of fear and depression for several weeks. Be careful what you allow to feed into your emotions.

7. Pray constantly. Don't get discouraged. Remain steadfast in prayer and as you spend time in fellowship with God, you will become more like Him. Pray regularly for those who disturb your emotional stability most (1 Thessalonians 5:17, Matthew 5:44).

8. Find support in the Body of Christ. We are to be an encouragement to each other in the Church. In order to be a help to each other we need to be open enough to allow others to bear our burdens with us (Hebrews 3:13 and 10:24).

9. Set your emotional rudder at the beginning of each day. Get on top of those uncontrolled emotions right at the start of your day. In your prayer time, set your heart to be forgiving, to be gentle, to be kind, and so forth. Each morning in prayer, I make "rudder declarations." I set my heart to have the heart of Christ (Matthew 6:9-13).

10. Praise God. Even if you do not feel like it, give God praise. Praise breaks the shackles of many emotional strongholds. Commit yourself to give praise to the Lord every day. Praise Him for His mercy and power. Praise Him for loving you and saving you (Philippians 4:4, 1 Thessalonians 5:18).

If you will determine to apply these ten Biblical principles you will discover a new control of your emotions. You will no longer experience an emotional roller-coaster plagued with fits of anger or depression.

Directly connected with our emotions are our actions. As mentioned earlier, many of our bad habits stem from emotional instability. I am confident that the application of the ten principles will bring you to a place of stability in your actions as well.

Discipline is a Key

Let me remind you that self-control often requires discipline and many of us are very undisciplined. We are quick to say that we want to be disciples of Jesus Christ, but we are slow to come under His discipline. I found my life out of control because there was little or no discipline in my Spiritual walk. Let me share with you three things I did to bring change. With these, I was able to move into an area of discipline and therefore self-control.

1. I accepted the blame for my lack of self-control. Don't blame others for your failure to be disciplined. I said my failure to exercise was because the Church kept me too busy. Overeating was because my wife is such a great cook. One man told me he couldn't quit smoking because of his children. Until we take responsibility for our choices, we will never move on to a place of discipline and self-control.

2. I began to make changes — gradually. Break those bad habits, but don't change everything at once. I have seen many fail to make changes because they quickly get discouraged when everything isn't changed at once.

Developing a prayer life happened very gradually for me. I began with just a few minutes three days a week. That prayer life has grown and is now a steady part of my daily routine.

3. Thirdly, I had to flee from evil. If you want to change bad habits, you have got to resist even being in situations of temptation.

I knew one woman struggling to lose weight who baked cookies every day. She needed to flee from sugar! Too often we set ourselves up for a fall simply by continuing to flirt with temptation!

As the Holy Spirit grows in you the fruit of self-control, add to it discipline and you will walk tall.

Questions For Discussion

1. Do you lack self-control? If so, can you talk about in what areas you would like to develop self-control?

2. Do you think the 10 biblical principles given in this chapter can help? Explain your answer.

3. Write on a separate piece of paper a bad habit or emotional instability you would like to put behind you. Collect them as a group and pray for each other to be encouraged to discover self-control. (You need not share what has been written.)

4. How can you break a bad habit — or how do you develop a good habit?

CHAPTER 7

Hanging Tough

. . . applying all diligence, in your faith, supply . . .
perseverance.

— 2 Peter 1:6

Have you ever noticed how often God uses our children to teach us life-lessons? Elaine and I are always learning from our four children. Rebekah had just turned one when she took her first solo steps at walking. She had tried prior to that, but had only experienced numerous crashes. This night, however, she tottered across the room with an enormous triumphant grin. Her persistence at learning to walk had paid off.

What if Rebekah had stopped trying to learn how to walk that very first time she fell? I'm sure it hurt a lot. There was security in crawling. If she had been fearful or had become easily discouraged, she might still be crawling today. Her desire to walk was so strong that she persevered, and now she walks.

I believe that some Christians never learn to stand — or to walk triumphantly — because they give up. They fail to persevere. If we are to walk without stumbling we must develop perseverance.

What is perseverance? It is steadfastness. It is persistence. When we look at the root meaning of the word we discover greater insight. Persevere is made up of two words: "Per," which denotes purpose, and "severe," which means just that, severe. To persevere is to remain faithful and steadfast in one's purpose in spite of severe opposition. Rebekah had received a vision of "walking." That vision became her goal or purpose — and in spite of various trials, she persisted toward that goal. Perseverance is not giving up when things get tough. It is tenaciously continuing to reach for the goal, vision or purpose set before us.

We find several examples of perseverance in the Bible:

> *There was in a certain city a judge who did not fear God,*
> *and did not respect man.*
> *And there was a widow in that city, and she kept coming*
> *to him, saying, "Give me legal protection from my*
> *opponent!"*

62

*And for a while he was unwilling, but afterward he said
to himself, "Even though I do not fear God nor respect
man,
yet because this woman bothers me, I will give her legal
protection lest by continually coming she wear me out."*
— Luke 18:2-5

The woman persisted until her goal was achieved.

In the Gospel of Matthew, chapter 15, we read of a Canaanite woman who came to Jesus, seeking to have her demon-possessed daughter healed. At first, Jesus put her off, but as she persisted, He healed her daughter.

The Apostle Paul certainly showed perseverance as he faced persecution, hardships and even death to take the gospel to the Gentiles. With clear purpose in mind, each of these remained steadfast.

Do you find yourself stumbling a lot in your Christian walk? Are there areas where you have given up, and now you believe you can never learn to stand in victory? Almost daily I observe Christians falling prey to sin, discouraged and doubtful that they can overcome. Pornography, sexual perversion, promiscuity, gambling, drunkenness, lust, bitterness, jealousy, outburst of anger, worry, gossip, rebellion, pride, greed — all these and more make up the plains of entrapment I see Christians crawling and falling in, failing to walk victoriously in the power of Jesus Christ.

If we will persevere we will stand. If we will not give up, no matter how severe the opposition, we can walk in triumph. There is no obstacle too big to overcome.

Not only is perseverance important in the realm of overcoming various sins, it is a crucial ingredient for the completion of tremendous achievements. How many times have we sensed God leading us to do something, but because there was some resistance, we quit. Where would the Church be today if the Apostle Paul had let stiff opposition hinder him from pioneering many Churches? What if Peter had heeded the Sanhedrin's orders and not spoken about Jesus anymore. Great accomplishments have been done for the Kingdom of God because men and women persevered to fulfill the call.

What has God called you to do and you failed to see it to fruition? Did you quit too soon? Because we have a natural tendency to avoid pain or conflict, many of us give up too quickly when opposition comes. We fail because we fail to add perseverance to our faith.

Allow me to offer a few perseverance pointers. Let these serve as anchors to enable you to "hang in there"— stick to it — stand and walk in victory.

Perseverance Pointers

1. You must have a clear sense of purpose. According to Proverbs 29:18, "Where there is no vision the people perish." Jesus, for the joy set before Him, endured the cross (Hebrews 12:2). We must have a clear vision of what we hope to accomplish, whether that is to overcome sin, or to fulfill some task. Without a clear sense of purpose or vision, we will not endure obstacles that will confront us.

2. We must be "God-dependent" to succeed. You do not persevere alone. We can do all things through Christ who strengthens us (Philippians 4:13). It is God who is at work in us to accomplish His will (Philippians 2:13). He who began a good work in you will perfect it until the day of Christ Jesus (Philippians 1:6).

A song that has encouraged and inspired me in times when I felt I could not go on is "In His Time." A portion of that song says, "In His time, He makes all things beautiful in His time." He is doing His work in us in His time. Rely on Him.

3. Have a support group to help you persevere. Hebrews 3:13 says, "Encourage one another day after day, as long as it is still called 'today,' lest any one of you be hardened by the deceitfulness of sin." God not only gave us the Helper to empower us, He gave us the helpers in the faith community to strengthen us. Do not hesitate to call upon trusted brothers and sisters in Christ to stand with you so that you can persevere.

4. Be willing to be held accountable. In seeking spiritual support, there must be a healthy measure of accountability allowed. Find a fellow believer who will hold you accountable in your endeavor to stand.

For many years I desired to keep a daily faith journal. Several unsuccessful attempts were made. The best I had ever done was eight consecutive days. I called upon a brother in Christ to hold me accountable. He was given permission to nag me about my journal-keeping. Just about every time he saw me he'd ask, "How's the journal coming?" I had to keep it up to date. He was a terrific brother to me and I now keep my faith-journal with steadfastness. My brother helped me persevere.

5. You have got to keep your guard up. Have you ever known someone who persevered, overcame some great obstacle in life, only to fall prey to it again years down the road? I have seen it many times. In a time of weakness, or mere negligence, sin crept in the door. The Apostle Peter certainly understood the potential of backsliding when he talked about sick dogs and muddy hogs. "It has happened to them according to the true proverb, 'A dog returns to its own vomit,' and 'A sow after washing, returns to wallowing in the mire' " (2 Peter 2:22).

We must keep our guard up if we are to persevere and not give Satan or sin a spiritual inch in our lives.

Remember in order to persevere, we must keep our vision clear. Rely upon Him to strengthen you. Stay in tight with your support group. Never get to the place where you think you no longer need the encouragement of others in the faith. Maintain accountability. While levels of accountability may change, there must always be some degree of being called into account. Don't let your guard down to give Satan opportunity.

It seems to me that perseverance is key to learning how to walk in victory. The times I have fallen have been times when I failed to persevere. I lost sight of my vision or purpose, or I began to rely upon my own strength. Too often I neglected to let the Church serve as both encourager and accounter and, therefore, I did not persevere. What a difference perseverance will make in the stability of our walk! Supply perseverance to your faith, and watch what happens.

Questions For Discussion

1. Can you talk about a time in your life when you failed to persevere?

2. Why do you think you failed to persevere?

3. Talk about your faith support group.

4. To whom are you accountable?

5. Discuss the importance of perseverance in our ability to walk the Christian walk.

CHAPTER 8

Growing In Godliness

. . . applying all diligence in your faith . . . supply . . .
godliness.

— 2 Peter 1:6

You've probably heard the expression, "He's so godly" or "She's such a godly woman." What do people mean when they describe someone as godly? Are we talking about someone who is very religious? Is there a piety about this man or woman that prompts us to label the person godly? What is godliness?

The word "godliness" literally means, "God-like-ness." There are in this Christian man or woman outstanding God-like characteristics that reflect God's nature to us. In other words, we see God in them. In this follower of Jesus we see actions and attitudes which mirror the Father's image. Are you godly? Is the quality of godliness increasing in you so that you will not be rendered fruitless? Are you being girded to stand and walk triumphantly by the growing fruit of godliness?

Is godliness obtainable? I have had Christians tell me that they didn't believe any of us can achieve godliness. These well-meaning brothers and sisters remind me that "we are only human"; therefore, we will continue to stumble and fall short of godliness. When we more fully understand what godliness is, and who we are as new creatures in Christ, we will understand that godliness is not only obtainable, but it is necessary for victorious Christian living.

Several years ago I heard a story about godliness that left a permanent impression on me.

> *One Sunday a little boy came home excited about the morning's lesson at Sunday School. He came bounding up to his father, who had stayed home reading the paper, anxious to tell his dad of what he had learned. "Daddy," he said, "today our teacher told us to live all this week just like Jesus. Do you think we can live like Jesus this week?"*
>
> *"No way!" his father spouted. "It would be impossible to be like Jesus for a week."*

"Well, Daddy, do you think we could live like Jesus for a day?"

"No, son," the father said frankly. "I don't believe we could live like Jesus for even a day."

"How about an hour?" the son asked timidly.

"I doubt it," replied the father.

"Daddy, do you suppose we could be like Jesus for just one minute? Do you think we could do that?"

"Well, I suppose we could live like Jesus for a minute," the father conceded.

"Do you think, Daddy, we could start today, living like Jesus just one minute at a time?"

— Source unknown

Godliness is a minute by minute quality of surrender to the Lordship of Jesus Christ in your life. Moment by moment He is transforming us. He is renewing our minds as Paul said in the letter to the Romans (Romans 12:2). The Father is conforming us to the image of His Son (Romans 8:29). Godliness is only possible as we turn daily to the right Source to obtain it.

The Road to Godliness

Godliness is a work of God, transforming us by the Holy Spirit, to be like our Heavenly Father. There is also responsibility on our part in this transformation process. We are commanded in Peter's first epistle:

> *Therefore, gird your minds for action, keep sober in spirit, fix your hope completely on the grace to be brought to you at the revelation of Jesus Christ.*
>
> *As obedient children, do not be conformed to the former lusts which were yours in your ignorance, but like the Holy One who called you, be holy in all your behavior; because it is written, "You shall be holy, for I am holy."*
> — 1 Peter 1:13-16

We have a role in this process of godliness. What are the steps on the road to godliness — the road that leads to standing firm in the faith?

Surrender

The first step toward godliness is surrender. Paul said, "I have been crucified with Christ; and it is no longer I who live, but Christ lives in me; and the life which I now live in the flesh I live by faith in the Son of God who loved me, and delivered Himself up for me" (Galatians 2:20). Obviously Paul had laid his life down, declaring Jesus as his Lord. It is when we turn our lives over to Jesus in full surrender that He is free to renew and transform completely. We are a new creation.

The tragic truth is, however, that we cling to some area of our lives that we refuse to submit to His Lordship. Too often Christians are crippled, unable to stand firm and walk in godliness because they have failed to submit all to Christ.

A few years ago I was visiting with a young teen Christian in his room. As we talked I couldn't help but notice the display of Christian posters, pictures of Christian entertainers, Bible verse flash cards and other symbols of this young man's faith. His bulletin board was covered with pictures of various Christian rock groups. In the lower right corner of his bulletin board I noticed one picture that just didn't fit. It was a photo of Motley Crew. I said, "What's this doing here?" He explained that once in a while he listened to them, too. (I think I should note here that Motley Crew has openly professed dabbling in the occult and have stated as one of their goals the demise of the family, fostering rebellion in teens.)

I shared with my young friend that his bulletin board was a reflection of the lives of many Christians. They want to be "gung-ho" for Jesus, but there is still one corner of ungodliness to which they cling. As long as we withhold from His Kingship any area of our lives, we will not enjoy the delight of godliness.

Knowing and Watching the Father

We cannot be "god-like" if we do not know what God is like. As we get to know God better, as our love grows deeper and more intimate with Him, we become more like Him. Spend time with Him. Be quiet before Him. Abide in His Word, witnessing His marvelous character with every page that you read.

In our congregation it is a custom that each Sunday one of our elders shares about an attribute of God. We call the time of sharing,

70

"Focus on the Father." It has been so refreshing to take a few moments each week and focus on God and His character.

I have noticed with our own children that as they hang out with Dad, they become like me (not always a blessing). Their vocabularies, inflections, even their mannerisms reflect their father, and mom, too! As we, the children of God, hang out with our heavenly Father, we will reflect Him.

Abide in the Blueprint Book

Time reading in the Bible enables us not only to see what God is like, but it shows us what we are to be like. The Bible serves as a spiritual mirror reflecting to us the image that pleases God. It challenges us to be radically different from those who do not profess to know Jesus as Lord. In Romans it says, "Do not be conformed to this world . . . ." (Romans 12:2). Conformed could be translated "shaped." We do not find our form or image reflected in the world but in the Word.

The Power of Prayer

I am convinced that without a serious, disciplined prayer life, one cannot achieve godliness that will lead to the ability to stand firm and walk confidently. You've probably heard the expression, "Prayer changes things." I agree, but I would change the "things" to "you." Prayer changes you! Prayer is not so much an exercise by which we convince God to change circumstances, but rather prayer is a fellowship by which we are transformed to line up to God's heart and will.

Jesus told us to pray for our enemies. Do you think that we were to pray that God would change them? Perhaps you think we were to pray that God would "squash" them? Every single time I have prayed for an enemy, I have been changed! My heart has been softened, finding a place of understanding, compassion and forgiveness for those who have transgressed against me. We become more "God-like" as we pray with an attitude of aligning ourselves up to God, rather than approaching Him to bend to His will.

71

Be on the Alert! Stay Spiritually Sensitized

Several times in Scripture we are commanded to be on the alert. I think that means to be sensitive to what is on God's heart, aware of what God is seeking to accomplish in us and in those around us. Being spiritually alert is being God-minded—God-like in our thoughts, attitudes and priorities.

When we look at the world through "God-colored glasses," we will see all things differently. We will see sin for all of its hideousness. Rather than looking down upon those who are without Christ as hopeless reprobates, we will view them as that lost lamb worthy of rescue. When trials come, we will rejoice at opportunities for growth rather than view them as cause for grumbling. Our entire view of human history and destiny will be radically transformed as we seek to understand it with the mind of Christ.

I served once on a panel debating the topic of abortion. I posed this question to one of the pro-choice advocates: "Do you believe that if a young woman who was considering abortion were to ask God what she should do, she would hear God say, 'Yes, kill the child'?" With red face the woman responded to me, "Frankly, I don't care what God might say!" This woman's position is a good example of why we miss godliness. We don't seek to know what God thinks or desires in various situations.

Ask God to help you see things as He does. Seek to have your heart tenderized to be as His heart. Be alert to the prompting of His Holy Spirit.

We can be like Him—more like Him each day. As we become more like Him, we become less like the world. The tugs of the flesh diminish and we find ourselves better prepared to stand when trials and temptations come. Certainly godliness is a key ingredient to our ability to stand.

Questions For Discussion

1. Can we achieve godliness? Explain your answer:

2. How do we know what God is like?

3. Do you enjoy a life-empowering prayer life? Discuss:

4. Is there any area of your life you have not surrendered to Him? Talk about it with the group:

5. How does godliness enable us to stand?

CHAPTER 9

Brotherly (And Sisterly) Kindness

. . . applying all diligence, in your faith, supply . . .
brotherly kindness . . .

— 2 Peter 1:6

I thought it was a typical youth meeting. We had played a game, sung some songs, spent some time in prayer and had entered into our Bible study. Just as we had begun to read the verses for that day, a girl shouted with reddened face to another, "I hate you!" The other young woman responded, "I hate you, too!" They both stomped out of the meeting screaming accusations at each other, ignoring my encouragement to stop and try to work things out.

There I stood before the rest of the group. They were silent and in shock. We paused and prayed for the two, then with much difficulty went on with our lesson. (Later I walked the girls through reconciliation.) The anger and vicious words of the two had unsettled the whole group. I understood what the author of Hebrews meant when he wrote, "See to it that no one comes short of the grace of God; that no root of bitterness springing up causes trouble and by it many be defiled" (Hebrews 12:15). I also saw first hand the importance of supplying brotherly kindness in our faith.

How does brotherly kindness fit in this list of Spiritual ingredients necessary for standing? Is there a correlation between our relationships with others and our relationship with God? Can our inability to be at peace with our fellow believers render us unable to stand, leaving us somehow spiritually crippled?

We often inflict wounds into one another in the Body of Christ because of our lack of brotherly kindness. Because of hurtful remarks or actions, I have seen many stumble due to broken embittered relationships. Brotherly kindness is essential to our ability to stand.

What is Brotherly Kindness?

Brotherly kindness is the condition by which we walk in relationship with fellow believers looking always to their edification and good. Paul, addressing the Christians at Ephesus (and us), encouraged them to walk in brotherly kindness. He wrote:

*Let no unwholesome word proceed from your mouth, but
only such a word as is good for edification according to
the need of the moment, that it may give grace to those
who hear.*
*And do not grieve the Holy Spirit of God by whom you
were sealed for the day of redemption.*
*Let all bitterness, and wrath and anger and clamor and
slander be put away from you along with all malice.*
*And be kind to one another, tender-hearted, forgiving
each other, just as God in Christ also has forgiven you.*
— Ephesians 4:29-32

Even when words of correction are given, they find their
inception in the motivation of edification for the individual and
the whole Body of Christ. Brotherly kindness cares about the
spiritual well-being of others, constantly seeking to enhance the
family of God.

Why is Brotherly Kindness So Important?

First of all, I believe that brotherly kindness is the evidence
that we really have found new life in Christ. "We know that we
have passed out of death into life, because we love the brethren.
He who does not love abides in death" (1 John 3:14).

I talked with a man one time who said he loved Jesus. He said
he was a devoted Christian, but that he did not attend Church. We
attempted to look at some biblical truths about the need for Christian
fellowship. He stopped me in the middle of a sentence and said,
"Hey, listen! I said I love Jesus. Don't you see . . . it's just Christians
I can't stand!" I found it difficult to believe that he really loved
Jesus, yet despised fellow Christians.

I believe that the Bible bears the truth, that those who love
Jesus will love His own. Our love for one another is a clear mark
of our life-changing relationship with Jesus Christ.

Secondly, our love for one another is our greatest witness to
the world. Jesus said, "By this all men will know that you are My
disciples, if you have love for one another" (John 13:35). It is
difficult to tell the world about the wonderful love of Christ when
they observe His followers inflicting painful wounds into one

another. Our deeds of love lavished upon one another speak far louder than any words we might offer, proclaiming that Christ does indeed live!

Thirdly, I believe brotherly kindness to be essential to our victorious walk because we know it to be the will of God. In Jesus' final prayer on planet Earth He prayed for unity in the Church. He prayed, "That they may all be one; even as Thou, Father, art in Me and I in Thee, that they also be in Us; that the world may believe that Thou didst send Me. And the glory which Thou has given Me I have given to them that they may be one, just as We are one . . ." (John 17:21-22).

If we are walking in a spirit of dissension, strife or bitterness, we are walking in conflict with the will of God. When we walk outside of the known will of God, we can expect only to stumble and fall. Walking in brotherly kindness is clearly His will.

Marks of Brotherly Kindness

The Bible gives us a clear picture of what it means to walk in brotherly kindness. To serve as a "spiritual check-up" consider the following expressions of brotherly kindness. Do these describe how you typically respond to brothers and sisters in Christ?

1. **Gentleness:** ". . . walk in a manner worthy of the calling with which you have been called, with all humility and gentleness, with patience, showing forbearance to one another in love" (Ephesians 4:1-2). Are you gentle with your brothers and sisters in Christ?

Our laundry detergent box proclaims that its contents are "gentle on all fabrics." That means it is not harsh, abrasive, nor does it cause colors to fade. Can the same be said of you in relation to all others in the Body of Christ? Gentleness is a tender attribute of brotherly kindness that does not diminish the glow of a brother or sister in Christ.

2. **Patience:** Paul said, "Love is patient and kind" (1 Corinthians 13:4). Many times in Scripture we are encouraged to be patient with one another. *Webster's New World Dictionary* says, "Patience is . . . the will or ability to wait or endure without complaint." As it directly relates to brotherly kindness, patience is the ability to wait

for a brother or sister to change without complaining or grumbling about his or her fault.

I can wait, but not always patiently! I have stood in line for long periods of time, but usually my waiting is accompanied with grumbling. The same is often true when it relates to fellow Christians. If I'm not careful and prayerful I can get impatient with their shortcomings. It's interesting; I expect them to be patient with me. In fact, I used to have a bumper sticker that said, "Be patient, God isn't finished with me yet." But too often I don't extend that same patient attitude to others.

Patience, accompanied with prayer, is a virtue of brotherly kindness that will not only enable you to stand tall, but will foster the same in your brothers and sisters in Christ. A thought that helps me is, "If God were to grant to me the same degree of patience that I am willing to grant to others, what kind of shape would I be in?" Probably dead!

3. **Proper Rebuke:** While we are called to be patient with one another, we are also called to speak correction to one another's lives. Jesus said, "Be on your guard! If your brother sins, rebuke him; and if he repents, forgive him" (Luke 17:3). Paul said to the Colossians, "Let the Word of Christ richly dwell within you, with all wisdom, teaching and *admonishing* one another with psalms and hymns and spiritual songs, singing with thankfulness in your hearts to God" (Colossians 3:16).

Brotherly kindness speaks words of correction with patient gentleness, with the hope to restore and edify a brother or sister. As admonitions are given for edification, both the giver and the recipient are equipped to be better able to stand! In fact, the whole Body of Christ is strengthened.

4. **Others First:** It is against our nature and in many ways against our culture to put others first. So much of what we hear and see advocates "look out for number one." Yet Paul wrote, "Do nothing from selfishness or empty conceit, but with humility of mind let each of you regard one another as more important than himself; do not merely look out for your own personal interests, but also for the interests of others" (Philippians 2:3-4).

Brotherly kindness that is "thee centered" rather than "me centered" will keep you standing tall.

5. **Generosity:** Francis of Assisi wrote, "It is in giving that we receive." How true that is! Generous giving opens up a tremendous channel of blessing into our lives enriching our ability to stand.

The early Christians made sure a fellow Christian never went without his or her needs met (Acts 2:45). They generously gave to see the Kingdom of God expanded. Brotherly kindness was expressed with concrete evidence to fellow believers—and to the world—as God's people gave.

6. **Encouragement:** Hebrews 3:13 says, "But encourage one another day after day, as long as it is still called 'today' lest any one of you be hardened by the deceitfulness of sin." The author of Hebrews knew how often we need encouragement. Every day! He also knew that without it our hearts can become hardened by sin. Brotherly kindness speaks words of encouragement to build up the Church.

One of the beautiful things about encouragement is that usually when you give it, it comes back to you and both the encourager and the "encouragee" stand taller! You do reap what you sow!

7. **Forgiving:** Ephesians 4:32 says, "And be kind to one another, tender-hearted, *forgiving* each other, just as God in Christ also has forgiven you." Brotherly kindness seeks to keep the slate clean, to hold no destructive grudges. Setting our will to forgive each day, no matter what the wrong suffered may be, will bring fresh power into our lives.

The world says, "Get even!" Just one evening of the news broadcast reveals that we live in a violent, vengeful world. That same evening news reveals that vengefulness never leads to life! As you set your heart to forgive, you will stand and walk in a joy and peace the world does not know.

In Summary

If you struggle in any one of these "brotherly-kindness-expressions," let me encourage you to turn to the one who gives us the ability to love one another. Turn to Jesus and ask Him to create in you a tender heart of love for fellow Christians. Perhaps it has been your nature to be unforgiving. Maybe you are just an impatient person. Encouragement may not come easy for you; you're too critical. You can change!

I believe that Jesus can and will transform us by the power of the Holy Spirit to live out brotherly kindness. We need an outpouring of love and gentle patience, encouragement and care in the Church today. Far too many are wounded and being wounded, while far too few are being nursed back to spiritual health.

The quality of brotherly kindness will not only enable you to walk in a new way, but you will be an enabler for others to walk in victory. What an essential ingredient brotherly kindness is to the ability to stand firm and to walk the Christian walk!

Questions For Discussion

1. What is brotherly kindness?

2. How do we develop brotherly kindness in our lives?

3. Describe a Church fellowship that is rich in brotherly kindness. Is your fellowship like that?

4. Is there an area of brotherly kindness that you find lacking in your own life? Can you share that with the group?

5. How can brotherly kindness enable us to stand and walk without stumbling, and even help others walk?

CHAPTER 10

Wrapped Up In Love

. . . applying all diligence, in your faith, supply . . . love!
— 2 Peter 1:6

Peter began with faith, and he wraps it up with love. Love is the glue that holds it all together. After all, without love we are a noisy gong or a clanging cymbal. Love is a vital ingredient to our ability to walk without stumbling. We must make love our aim (1 Corinthians 14:1).

The Nature of Love
Love is far more than an emotion. It is a choice. It is a commitment. It is even a sacrifice. When the Scripture says that "God so loved the world," it does not mean that he just felt a warm, fuzzy feeling for us. It means he sovereignly chose, out of His commitment to His creation, to sacrifice His only Son for us. Too often we love only when we feel like it, rather than walking in true biblical love. Love is laying our lives down for others, loving the unlovely, binding up the broken and healing the hurting.

Christian love begins in knowing that we ourselves are loved. One who does not know the love and mercy of God personally is incapable of loving others as he or she should. Perhaps due to past sins, or a painful childhood, or even negative encounters in the church, you may find it difficult to believe that you are loved by God. There is nothing so awful that you have done that His forgiveness cannot cover it! There is no hurt so deep that His grace cannot heal it. And there is no bitterness so vile that His cleansing power cannot wash it. Receive His love and at the same time receive the ability to love others.

Love is the Fruit of the Spirit
Because Christian love is dependent upon more than emotions, we must look beyond ourselves for its source. God is the beginning and the end of genuine love!

According to the Apostle Paul in Galatians, chapter five, the fruit of the Spirit is love. Love is a natural by-product of the indwelling power of the Spirit of God in one's life. As we daily surrender to the Holy Spirit, the love of God is lived out through us.

Galatians chapter 5 does reveal some keen insights to the nature of the fruit of love. Paul wrote:

> *But the fruit of the Spirit is love, joy, peace, patience, kindness, goodness, faithfulness, gentleness, self-control; against such things there is no law.*
>
> — Galatians 5:22-23

I've seen plaques in Christian bookstores and I've heard many Christians refer to these verses as "the fruits of the Holy Spirit." I believe Paul intentionally used the singular in order to clearly say, "The *fruit* of the Spirit is Love." The other character qualities in Paul's list are the results or further definition of love. Let me illustrate what I mean by a cross-reference to Paul's letter to the Corinthians in which He described real Love. He wrote:

> *Love is patient, love is kind, and is not jealous; love does not brag and is not arrogant, does not act unbecomingly, it does not seek its own, is not provoked, does not take into account a wrong suffered, does not rejoice in unrighteousness, but rejoices with the truth; bears all things, believes all things, hopes all things, endures all things. Love never fails . . . .*
>
> — 1 Corinthians 13:4-8a

Do you see the connection? The Fruit of the Spirit is love, which results in . . .

Joy	"Love rejoices with the truth!"
Peace	"Love bears, believes, hopes all things."
Patience	"Love is patient."
Kindness	"Love is kind."
Goodness	"Love does not act unbecomingly."
Faithfulness	"Love endures all things . . . never fails."

Gentleness	"Love is not jealous, does not brag, does not take into account a wrong suffered."
Self-control	"Love is not provoked . . . does not seek its own."

I say "Amen" to Paul's encouragement that we "make love our aim." Spirit-produced-love will enable us to stand and walk in great joy!

While we cannot produce this love, we can help it grow. We can provide nourishment and water to this fruit by abiding in and submitting to the Word of God. We can enable this fruit to be enlarged and sweetened by basking in the Son, enjoying His presence through worship and prayer. Love comes from Him and increases in us as we daily grow closer to Him.

How is Love Lived Out?

Sacrifice: Love is lived out in sacrifice. God set the example for us in the supreme sacrifice of His Son. Jesus said, "Greater love has no one than this, that one lay down his life for his friends" (John 15:13). Being sacrificial in our love toward others does not merely mean being willing to die for them. It means being willing to live and give for them. It means meeting that confused college student at the coffee shop at 2 a.m. to give a listening ear and counsel. It means not buying that new dress so you can pay the utility bill of that single mom struggling to make ends meet. Genuine love is sacrificial.

Commitment: Genuine love is a commitment, not just a feeling. I had a couple who wanted to change the wedding vows from "as long as we both shall live" to "as long as we both shall love." What they were striving to do was to give each other permission to terminate the relationship if or when the "feelings" of love stopped.

Real love is commitment that goes beyond feelings. In the Church, that love commitment means that I keep on loving even if we disagree about some things . . . or even if you hurt me.

Humility: Humility is a mark of Godly love. It is not condescending. It approaches each person as "fearfully and wonderfully made" (Psalm 139:14). Genuine love causes us to be ever conscious of the needs and desires of others. There is great power in the ability to look upon others as Christ does, through humble, gentle eyes of compassion. Too often pride is a stumbling block that prevents us from loving others as we ought.

Obedience: Jesus said, "If you love me you will keep my commandments" (John 14:15). He also said that the greatest commandment was to love God and to love our neighbor. Failure to love is disobedience. Disobedience is failure to love Christ fully. There are times we are to walk in love, regardless of circumstances or emotions, simply because it is our Lord's directive. If nothing else, we choose to love out of love for Him!

Action: Love is lived out by outward expressions. James wrote, "Faith without works is dead" (James 2:26b). I would say, "Love without action is a lie!" We can daily take delight in touching, giving, caring, and listening to enhance the lives of others. God has given us our circle of family, friends and acquaintances upon whom to live out the expressions of His love. Let us seize every opportunity to love.

WITHOUT CHRIST, WE CANNOT LOVE
WITHOUT LOVE, WE CANNOT STAND

Love enables us to walk without stumbling . . .

* because we are daily giving ourselves to enrich the lives of others
* because we hold a firm commitment to walk in a nurture-giving relationship with others
* because we humbly approach every person as a precious creation of God
* because we seek to walk in obedience to Him, relating to one another as we would relate to Him
* because we daily fill our lives seeking out ways to express the love that is in us!

Love enables us to walk without stumbling . . . !!!

The previous principles Peter has given have no worth if they are not motivated by the consuming fires of love. If we do not love, we are a noisy gong! If love is not our driving force as we walk the Christian walk, we will certainly stumble and fall. John said it best in one of his little epistles:

Beloved, let us love one another, for love is from God; and everyone who loves is born of God and knows God. The one who does not love does not know God, for God is love.

— 1 John 4:7-8

Bear the fruit of love, and you will walk in confident delight!

Questions For Discussion

1. Whom do you find it most difficult to love?

2. How can we "grow" the fruit of love?

3. What inhibits us from loving as we ought?

4. List several ways we can express love: (concrete action!)

5. Why is the quality of love such a critical ingredient to our ability to walk without stumbling?

Walking with the One Who Makes You Able to Stand

Now to Him who is able to keep you from stumbling,
and to make you stand in the presence of His glory
blameless with great joy, to the only God our Savior,
through Jesus Christ our Lord, be glory, majesty,
dominion and authority, before all time and now and
forever. Amen. — Jude 24

We cannot stand on our own. It is only in and through Christ Jesus that we are able to stand. Do you know Jesus Christ as your Savior and friend? Do you stand in confidence as one who has been fully forgiven and assured an eternal home in heaven?

Our Heavenly Father made knowing Him, and becoming a recipient of His eternal gift very simple . . . as simple as **ABC**.

A=Acknowledge you are a sinner in need of a Savior (Romans 3:23, 1 John 1:9).
B=Believe that Jesus died and rose again for your salvation (John 3:16, 1 John 5:11-13).
C=Confess Jesus as your Lord (Romans 10:8-11).

Simply tell God you are sorry for your sins, and thank Him for sending His Son to die in your place. Repent, or turn from any sin that you know of in your life that is not pleasing to God. Put your trust (believe) in what Jesus has done for you on the cross. Invite Him to come into your life and change your life, as Lord of your life. And now, tell someone that Jesus is now Lord of your life.

CHAPTER 11

Able To Stand

If these qualities are yours . . . .   — 2 Peter 1:8

I believe that the Spirit of God sovereignly led me to these verses in Second Peter to show me how to stand and how to walk. My life up until that time had been characterized by frequent stumbling and frustration. That all changed when I realized the provisions God had put in place to enable me to stand. And it can change for you!

Building Blocks to Stand

Peter, inspired by the Holy Spirit, has given us building blocks for a life of stability and peace. Upon the foundation of our faith in Christ, we lay the brick of moral excellence. Faith without works is dead! And faith that is not accompanied with a passion to do what is pleasing to the Lord is probably counterfeit.

Upon the brick of moral excellence, we add knowledge. If we do not know Him, His will and His ways, we cannot achieve moral excellence. The Pharisees sought moral excellence apart from knowing God, and it only led to legalism and hypocrisy.

The brick of self-control rests securely on top of knowledge. Knowing God does transform us, yet we must remember that we have responsibility in this life-changing process. We must choose to have things differently. We must add self-control to our relationship with Him.

Does self-control require perseverance? You bet! I have known folks who have quit smoking dozens of times. Don't give up! While you may not overcome whatever it is that entangles you instantly, add perseverance to self-control and you will overcome.

To that perseverance, lay the brick of godliness. It's not mere "bull-headedness" that will see you to victory. It is "God-headedness." It is a desire to be like your heavenly Father, to bring honor to him. Perseverance can only produce its fullest fruit as we are willing to submit to God-in-us to change us.

Godliness must be tempered by the brick of brotherly kindness. We must grant patience, kindness and compassion to one another in the Body of Christ to see godliness accomplished. As we encourage one another daily in brotherly kindness, we see the character of God come forth in us.

Above all, we are called to mortar in the brick of love. Love is essential. If we could walk in the seven previous principles, yet lacked love, we would be a noisy gong or clanging cymbal. Love confirms that God is in us changing us. Love draws the world to Jesus Christ!

What a powerful effect it will have on our lives to claim these qualities as our own! We will be able to stand and to walk in newness of life!

"If these qualities are yours and are increasing . . . ."

After Peter has given us these eight essential qualities necessary to enable us to walk without stumbling, he gives some words of caution and encouragement.

Growing on: Peter reminds us that these qualities must be increasing. As we have submitted our lives to Christ and have received the Holy Spirit, each of these qualities has been apportioned to us in some measure. Therefore we can say with confidence that we have faith, moral excellence, knowledge, self-control, perseverance, godliness, brotherly kindness and love. We cannot, however, claim to possess any of these qualities in fullest measure. They must be increasing.

God is daily growing us. We are being transformed and renewed. We are being conformed to the image of Christ. As we continue to seek after Him we will see these qualities increase and as they increase we will see our fruitfulness enlarged.

Fine fruit: Peter wrote, "For if these qualities are yours and are increasing, they render you neither useless nor unfruitful in the true knowledge of our Lord Jesus Christ" (2 Peter 1:8). I want my life to count for God's kingdom. Don't you? I want to be fruitful and useful for Him. If these qualities are increasing in us good fruit is produced!

As our faith increases we walk in a peace and security the world cannot understand. Many will be drawn to Christ as they see us enjoying the peace He gives by faith. Firm faith gives us the ability to offer wise counsel and bring edification and encouragement to the Body of Christ.

The increase of moral excellence enhances our witness. Because the world sees a difference in us, they are more ready to believe our testimony. Moral excellence is also liberating. We enjoy a clear conscience before God and men. We sleep well at night. We are free from the bondage and consequences of sins which once entangled us.

Our knowledge of Him, His promises and His will causes us to be a pointer for others to know Him, too. We walk in a new confidence as we know His will, seeing Him accomplish what He has purposed for us. We don't waste our time doing things He didn't design us to do, therefore we are more productive.

We are spared many ugly entanglements because self-control is growing in us. We don't "blow up" anymore, therefore we avoid senseless painful arguments. We are not easily swayed by our emotions into fear or depression, therefore we are more usable and available to minister help to others. Disciplined self-control has brought delight into our lives.

We're not quitters! The one who finishes the race gets the prize. The quality of perseverance is growing in us, therefore we are seeing the works He began in us to fruition. We aren't easily disturbed by adversity because we are confident in the vision and provision God has put before us.

We are children of God growing up to be more like our Father. Because of that truth, more of the Father's fruit is seen in our lives. Our godliness reflects Him, and others are drawn to the light of His love.

Church fights aren't our thing! We are peacemakers. Walking and growing in the quality of brotherly kindness, we are bringing edification to the Body of Christ. Therefore the witness of the whole Church is enhanced.

We are Godly lovers! Laying our lives down for others, we see our realm of ministry enriched with fresh, changed lives daily. No one can resist *real* love! The world will know we truly are His as we grow in the quality of love.

If these qualities are ours and are increasing we will be useful and fruitful. We'll make a powerful difference upon the world in which we live. Not only that, we will enjoy a rich walk with Christ — *no stumbling included!*

A Word of Caution

Peter does give us a word of warning. He wrote, "For he who lacks these qualities is blind or short-sighted, having forgotten his purification from his former sins. Therefore, brethren, be all the more diligent to make certain about His calling and choosing you; for as long as you practice these things, you will never stumble" (2 Peter 1:9-10).

He reminds us that if we lack these qualities we are blind or short-sighted. We have forgotten what Jesus did for us when he died on Calvary.

If these qualities are lacking in our lives, we will never see as we ought. What happens to persons who cannot see well when they try to walk? They stumble!

Blindness or shortsightedness generally comes when we forget about the cross. We can become self-reliant, callous to sin, even arrogant if we forget that Jesus had to die! Excuse the pun, but in the spiritual realm the only one who can see clearly is the one who is *cross*-eyed. We must always remember the cross. Without the cross, there would be no sacrifice for sin. Without the Blood of the Lamb of God, there would be no cleansing from sin's stain.

Peter also reminds us to be certain of our call and God's choosing us. We confirm our call by practicing these things — the eight qualities — we have been discussing. And as we practice them, we can walk in the assurance that we will not stumble.

When you accepted Christ you began a wonderful journey. You received the invitation to walk in new confidence and stability. Some Christians are still crawling. Far too many are constantly stumbling, inflicting painful wounds to themselves and to others. Many, however, are finding a grand victorious walk of security, peace and joy. How about you? Let's learn to walk without stumbling, allowing God to increase His qualities in us so that we might bear much fruit!

Questions For Discussion

1. What is the significance of the progression of these eight qualities in Scripture from faith to love. Do they build upon each other?

2. Why is it important that these qualities be increasing?

3. How do these qualities affect the whole Church?

4. What if we lack these qualities?

5. What does it mean to be blind or short-sighted spiritually?

6. How can we be careful to keep our focus on the cross?

7. What does it mean to practice these qualities?

8. Are you going to walk without stumbling?